Officers Everywhere!

Written by Charnan Simon • Illustrated by Ronnie Rooney

Published in the United States of America by The Child's World®
PO Box 326 • Chanhassen, MN 55317-0326
800-599-READ • www.childsworld.com

Reading Adviser

Cecilia Minden-Cupp, PhD, Former Language and Literacy Program Director,
Harvard Graduate School of Education, Cambridge, Massachusetts

Acknowledgments

The Child's World®: Mary Berendes, Publishing Director

Editorial Directions, Inc.: E. Russell Primm, Editorial Director and Project Manager;
Katie Marsico, Associate Editor; Judith Shiffer, Assistant Editor; Caroline Wood, Editorial Assistant

The Design Lab: Kathleen Petelinsek, Design and Art Production

Library of Congress Cataloging-in-Publication Data

Simon, Charnan.
   Officers everywhere! / written by Charnan Simon ; illustrated by Ronnie Rooney.
     p. cm. — (Magic door to learning)
   ISBN 1-59296-626-8 (library bound : alk. paper) 1. Police—Juvenile literature. I. Rooney,
Ronnie, ill. II. Title. III. Series.
   HV7922.S55 2007
   363.2—dc22   2006001631

A book is a door, a magic door.
It can take you places
you have never been before.
Ready? Set?
Turn the page.
Open the door.
Now it is time to explore.

Early in the morning and late
at night, police officers everywhere
are ready to help!

Some officers work in patrol cars. They drive slowly up and down the street, making sure everyone is safe.

Some officers stay in
the police station. They
answer the telephones
when people call for help.

Police officers work in all kinds
of weather! They sometimes
help direct traffic.

They help when kittens
get stuck in trees.

Police work can be dangerous.

Police work can be fun.

Some officers work
with dogs. Police
dogs use their
sense of smell to
find lost children.

Some officers ride horses.
Police horses keep parades in line.

Police officers are everywhere—and they are always ready to help people!

Our story is over, but there is still much to explore beyond the magic door!

Did you know that you can help police officers take care of your neighborhood? Get together with your friends and make a list of ten things you can do to keep the area safe. One idea is walking to and from school in groups of three or more. Another possibility is naming three or four adults in your neighborhood who you could go to for help during an emergency. At the bottom of your list, write the non-emergency phone number of the police station. (Be sure to dial 9-1-1 if there's ever a real emergency.)

These books will help you explore at the library and at home:

Hayward, Linda. *A Day in the Life of a Police Officer.* New York: DK Publishing, 2001.

Rathmann, Peggy. *Officer Buckle and Gloria.* New York: Putnam, 1995.

About the Author

Charnan Simon lives in Madison, Wisconsin, where she can usually be found sitting at her desk and writing books, unless she is sitting at her desk and looking out the window. Charnan has one husband, two daughters, and two very helpful cats.

About the Illustrator

Ronnie Rooney studied painting at the University of Massachusetts at Amherst. She received a degree in illustration at the Savannah College of Art and Design in Georgia. She spends most of her time drawing and painting . . . but she occasionally heads to the beach to play in the sand.